MW01714120

THE ORIGIN OF THE DON SPHYNX CAT BREED 3

PHYSICAL CHARACTERISTICS OF THE DON SPHYNX CAT 6

TEMPERAMENT AND PERSONALITY TRAITS OF DON SPHYNX CATS 8

DON SPHYNX CARE AND GROOMING 11

DON SPHYNX HEALTH AND LIFESPAN 14

DON SPHYNX DIET AND NUTRITION 16

DON SPHYNX EXERCISE AND PLAY 19

DON SPHYNX SOCIALIZATION 22

DON SPHYNX AS FAMILY PETS 25

DON SPHYNX ALLERGIES: MISCONCEPTIONS AND FACTS 28

DON SPHYNX BREEDING AND REPRODUCTION 31

DON SPHYNX BREEDER SELECTION 34

DON SPHYNX KITTENS: CARE AND MANAGEMENT 37

DON SPHYNX ADOPTION: CONSIDERATIONS AND PROCESS 40

DON SPHYNX TRAINING TIPS 43

DON SPHYNX CAT SHOWS: AN OVERVIEW 46

DON SPHYNX BREED STANDARDS: AN IN-DEPTH EXAMINATION 48

DON SPHYNX CLOTHING AND ACCESSORIES: ENHANCING COMFORT AND WELL-BEING 51

DON SPHYNX ART AND CULTURE: A SCIENTIFIC EXPLORATION 54

DON SPHYNX CATS IN DIFFERENT COUNTRIES: A CROSS-CULTURAL EXAMINATION 57

DON SPHYNX CAT MYTHS AND MISCONCEPTIONS: A SCIENTIFIC CLARIFICATION 60

DON SPHYNX RESCUE AND ADVOCACY: A SCIENTIFIC OVERVIEW 63

DON SPHYNX AND OTHER PETS: SCIENTIFIC GUIDANCE ON INTRODUCTION 65

DON SPHYNX GENETIC HEALTH TESTING: ENSURING BREED HEALTH THROUGH SCIENTIFIC EVALUATION 68

DON SPHYNX COMMUNITY AND ONLINE FORUMS: CONNECTING ENTHUSIASTS SCIENTIFICALLY 71

DON SPHYNX STORIES AND ANECDOTES: A SCIENTIFIC LOOK AT HEARTWARMING TALES 73

DON SPHYNX CAT CARE RESOURCES: SCIENTIFICALLY CURATED REFERENCES 76

DON SPHYNX ART AND PHOTOGRAPHY: A SCIENTIFIC EXPLORATION OF AESTHETIC EXPRESSIONS 78

DON SPHYNX AND THE FUTURE: A SCIENTIFIC SPECULATION 80

DON SPHYNX'S ENDEARING QUALITIES: A SCIENTIFIC SUMMARY 82

THE ORIGIN OF THE DON SPHYNX CAT BREED

INTRODUCTION

The Don Sphynx, also known as the Don Hairless or Russian Hairless, is a distinctive cat breed renowned for its hairless appearance. This breed's history is intriguing and offers insights into its origins, development, and unique characteristics. In this scientific exploration, we delve into the origin and history of the Don Sphynx cat breed.

EARLY DEVELOPMENT

The history of the Don Sphynx begins in Russia during the early 20th century. Contrary to some misconceptions, the breed is not a product of selective breeding to create a hairless cat but rather the result of a naturally occurring genetic mutation. The first recorded sighting of a hairless cat in Russia dates back to the early 20th century, although the exact year remains uncertain.

DISCOVERY AND INITIAL BREEDING

The Don Sphynx's development can be attributed to the discovery of these hairless cats in the Russian Rostov-on-Don region, thus giving the breed its name. These cats were found in the streets and were gradually integrated into local households. As they possessed a distinctive appearance, breeders became interested in understanding the genetic basis of their hairlessness.

GENETIC MUTATION

Scientific investigations revealed that the hairlessness of the Don Sphynx is caused by a naturally occurring genetic mutation affecting the development of hair follicles. This mutation, referred to as the hr gene (hairless gene), leads to the absence of a proper coat. Breeders recognized the potential of this unique genetic trait and began selective breeding to establish a stable breed with consistent hairlessness.

EARLY BREEDING EFFORTS

Early breeding efforts faced challenges as the breed's gene pool was limited to the cats found in the Rostov-on-Don region. These cats were crossbred with other breeds, including Siamese and Russian Blue, to diversify the gene pool and enhance the breed's overall health and temperament. This period of experimentation and crossbreeding laid the foundation for the modern Don Sphynx.

RECOGNITION AND STANDARDIZATION

The Don Sphynx breed gained recognition in Russia in the mid-20th century. In 1987, it was officially recognized by the Russian Ministry of Agriculture. However, international recognition took more time to materialize. The breed's unique appearance and charming personality eventually led to its acceptance by major cat breed registries, such as The International Cat Association (TICA) and the Cat Fanciers' Association (CFA).

MODERN DON SPHYNX

Today, the Don Sphynx is a well-established breed known for its distinctive hairlessness, almond-shaped eyes, and friendly disposition. Breeders have successfully maintained the breed's genetic diversity while preserving its unique appearance and character.

CONCLUSION

The Don Sphynx's origin is rooted in a natural genetic mutation found in the Rostov-on-Don region of Russia. Through careful breeding and genetic selection, this unique and captivating breed has evolved into the recognizable and cherished feline companion it is today. Its history exemplifies the fascinating interplay between genetics, human intervention, and the development of distinctive cat breeds.

PHYSICAL CHARACTERISTICS OF THE DON SPHYNX CAT

COAT AND SKIN

The Don Sphynx is renowned for its distinctive hairless appearance, which sets it apart from most other cat breeds. However, despite its name, the breed is not entirely devoid of hair. The Don Sphynx possesses a fine layer of downy, peach-fuzz-like hair covering its body, giving it a unique texture. This minimal coat provides a velvety feel to the touch, and it may vary in color and pattern, much like traditional cat fur. Don Sphynx cats are often found in a wide array of coat colors and patterns, including solid, tabby, bicolor, and more.

BODY SHAPE AND SIZE

The Don Sphynx exhibits a distinctive and striking body shape. It is a medium to large-sized cat breed with a robust and muscular build. Key physical characteristics of the Don Sphynx's body include: Head: The head is wedge-shaped with prominent cheekbones and a flat skull. The breed features defined cheek ruffs and prominent whisker pads. Ears: The Don Sphynx's ears are large, wide at the base, and often have rounded tips. They stand upright and contribute to the breed's alert and expressive appearance. Eyes: This breed boasts large, almond-shaped eyes set at a slight angle. Eye color varies but is typically in shades of green or gold, although blue and amber hues are also possible. Neck: The Don Sphynx has a long and sturdy neck, which blends seamlessly into its body. Torso: The breed's torso is muscular and well-defined, with a prominent chest and a deep ribcage. The back is straight, and the abdomen is slightly rounded. Legs: Don Sphynx cats have long, slender legs that are proportionate to their body size. The paws are oval-shaped with prominent knuckles. Tail: The tail of the Don Sphynx is long and tapering, with a slight curve. It is flexible and can be expressive, often reflecting the cat's mood.

SKIN CARE

Due to their lack of traditional fur, Don Sphynx cats require special care to maintain their skin health. Their exposed skin is prone to temperature fluctuations, making them sensitive to extreme heat and cold. Owners must protect them from sunburn in hot weather and ensure they stay warm in colder conditions. Regular bathing is essential to remove excess oils from their skin and prevent a buildup of debris. Additionally, Don Sphynx cats are prone to skin conditions like rashes, sores, and infections, making routine skin examinations crucial. In conclusion, the Don Sphynx's unique physical characteristics, including its distinctive coat, body shape, and size, make it a visually captivating breed. While its hairlessness sets it apart, the breed's skin care requirements highlight the importance of responsible ownership and diligent maintenance to ensure the well-being of these captivating feline companions.

TEMPERAMENT AND PERSONALITY TRAITS OF DON SPHYNX CATS

INTRODUCTION

The Don Sphynx, known for its unique hairless appearance, is not only distinctive in its physical characteristics but also in its temperament and personality. Understanding the behavioral traits of this breed is essential for potential owners and enthusiasts. In this scientific exploration, we delve into the temperament and personality traits of Don Sphynx cats.

SOCIAL AND AFFECTIONATE

Don Sphynx cats are renowned for their social and affectionate nature. They form strong bonds with their human companions and thrive on attention and interaction. These cats are often described as "people-oriented" and enjoy being the center of attention in the household. They are known to follow their owners around, eager to engage in play and cuddle sessions.

CURIOUS AND PLAYFUL

This breed exhibits a high level of curiosity and playfulness. Don Sphynx cats are known for their inquisitive nature and love to explore their environment. They are particularly fond of interactive toys and puzzles that challenge their intelligence. Providing mental and physical stimulation is essential to keep them engaged and content.

TALKATIVE

Don Sphynx cats are known to be vocal and expressive. They are not shy about sharing their thoughts and desires with their human companions. While they may not be as loud as some other breeds, they are skilled in using a wide range of vocalizations, including purring, chirping, and meowing, to communicate their needs and emotions.

FRIENDLY AND EXTROVERTED

Extroverted by nature, Don Sphynx cats are typically friendly and outgoing. They are known to get along well with other pets, including dogs and other cats, if properly introduced. Their social disposition makes them a great choice for households with multiple animals, as they often enjoy the company of their furry companions.

WARM AND AFFECTIONATE

Don Sphynx cats have a warm and affectionate temperament. They are known to seek physical contact and warmth, often cuddling with their owners to share body heat. This behavior is especially prominent in cooler environments due to their lack of fur.

INTELLIGENT AND PROBLEM-SOLVING

This breed is recognized for its intelligence and problem-solving abilities. Don Sphynx cats enjoy mental challenges and are quick learners. Puzzle toys and interactive games that engage their minds are excellent choices for stimulating their intellect.

CONCLUSION

In conclusion, Don Sphynx cats are unique not only in their appearance but also in their temperament and personality traits. Their social, affectionate, and intelligent nature makes them beloved companions for individuals and families alike. Understanding and catering to their specific needs and preferences is essential for providing a happy and fulfilling life for these extraordinary feline companions.

DON SPHYNX CARE AND GROOMING

INTRODUCTION

Caring for a Don Sphynx cat, known for its distinctive hairless appearance, requires special attention to its unique coat and skin. This scientific guide outlines the essential grooming and care practices to ensure the well-being of Don Sphynx cats.

BATHING AND SKIN CARE

Due to the absence of traditional fur, Don Sphynx cats require regular bathing to maintain skin health. Here are the key steps for effective skin care: Frequency: Bathe your Don Sphynx regularly, typically every 1 to 2 weeks. However, the frequency may vary depending on the cat's activity level and exposure to dirt and oil. Water Temperature: Use lukewarm water to prevent shocking the cat's sensitive skin. Ensure that the bathing environment is warm and comfortable. Gentle Shampoo: Choose a mild, hypoallergenic cat shampoo. Avoid human shampoos or products with harsh chemicals, as they can irritate the skin. Thorough Rinse: Rinse the shampoo thoroughly to remove all residue, as any leftover soap can lead to skin irritation. Drying: Gently pat the cat dry with a soft, absorbent towel. Avoid vigorous rubbing to prevent skin abrasion. Moisturizing: Apply a veterinarian-recommended, hypoallergenic moisturizer to keep the skin supple and prevent dryness. Be sure to use products specifically designed for cats.

TEMPERATURE CONSIDERATIONS

Don Sphynx cats are sensitive to temperature changes due to their lack of fur. Ensure they are comfortable by following these guidelines: Warmth: Provide a warm environment, especially in cooler climates. Use heating pads or blankets, and keep your home at a comfortable temperature. Sun Protection: Protect your Don Sphynx from direct sunlight, as their exposed skin is susceptible to sunburn. Use pet-safe sunscreen or provide shade when outdoors. Cooling in Summer: During hot weather, provide access to a cool, shaded area and fresh water to prevent overheating.

EAR AND EYE CARE

Don Sphynx cats have large ears and eyes that require special attention: Ear Cleaning: Clean the ears regularly with a veterinarian-approved ear cleaner and cotton balls to prevent wax buildup and infections. Avoid using cotton swabs, which can push debris deeper into the ear canal. Eye Cleaning: Wipe the eyes with a damp, soft cloth to remove any discharge. Be gentle to avoid irritating the sensitive eye area.

NAIL TRIMMING

Regular nail trimming is essential to prevent overgrowth and discomfort for both the cat and its human companions. Use cat-specific nail clippers and be cautious not to cut too close to the quick.

DIET AND NUTRITION

A balanced diet is vital for maintaining the Don Sphynx's overall health. Consult with a veterinarian to choose a suitable cat food that meets their specific dietary requirements, including any skin and coat supplements if recommended.

CONCLUSION

In conclusion, caring for a Don Sphynx cat involves unique considerations due to their hairless coat and sensitive skin. Regular bathing, temperature management, and specialized grooming practices are crucial for their well-being. With proper care, Don Sphynx cats can enjoy a happy and healthy life, showcasing their distinctive and captivating appearance.

DON SPHYNX HEALTH AND LIFESPAN

INTRODUCTION

Understanding the health considerations and typical lifespan of the Don Sphynx breed is essential for responsible ownership. This scientific overview explores common health issues and the expected lifespan of Don Sphynx cats.

COMMON HEALTH ISSUES

While Don Sphynx cats are generally healthy, they are prone to certain health issues, some of which are associated with their unique hairless characteristics: Skin Conditions: Due to their lack of fur, Don Sphynx cats are susceptible to various skin issues, including rashes, fungal infections, and sunburn. Regular skin care and protection are essential to prevent these problems. Respiratory Issues: The breed is prone to upper respiratory infections, similar to other cats. Proper vaccination and a clean living environment can help reduce the risk. Heart Disease: Don Sphynx cats may be at a higher risk of hypertrophic cardiomyopathy (HCM), a genetic heart condition. Regular veterinary check-ups can help monitor heart health. Gastrointestinal Issues: Some Don Sphynx cats may have sensitive stomachs and are prone to digestive problems. A balanced diet and proper feeding schedule are important. Dental Health: Dental issues, such as gingivitis and periodontal disease, can occur. Regular dental care, including brushing, can help maintain oral hygiene.

LIFESPAN

The typical lifespan of a Don Sphynx cat is similar to that of other domestic cats, ranging from 12 to 15 years on average. With attentive care, a healthy diet, regular veterinary check-ups, and a suitable living environment, some Don Sphynx cats have been known to live beyond 15 years. It's important to note that genetics, lifestyle, and proper healthcare play significant roles in determining an individual cat's lifespan. Early detection and treatment of health issues through routine veterinary care can contribute to a longer and healthier life for Don Sphynx cats.

CONCLUSION

In conclusion, while the Don Sphynx breed is generally healthy, they do have specific health considerations related to their hairlessness and genetics. Regular veterinary care, attention to their unique needs, and a well-balanced lifestyle can help ensure that Don Sphynx cats lead fulfilling lives and achieve their expected lifespan. Responsible ownership and early intervention for health issues are key factors in promoting the well-being of this captivating and unique breed.

DON SPHYNX DIET AND NUTRITION

INTRODUCTION

Proper diet and nutrition are fundamental to the health and well-being of Don Sphynx cats, especially due to their unique hairless characteristics. This scientific guide provides nutritional recommendations tailored to the specific needs of Don Sphynx cats.

SPECIAL DIETARY CONSIDERATIONS

Don Sphynx cats have some distinct dietary considerations related to their hairless coat and metabolism: High-Energy Requirements: Don Sphynx cats tend to have higher energy requirements than some other breeds. Their lack of fur means they expend more energy to maintain body temperature. A diet with appropriate calorie content is crucial to meet their energy needs. Skin Health: The breed's hairless nature makes their skin more vulnerable to external factors. To promote healthy skin, provide a diet rich in essential fatty acids, such as omega-3 and omega-6, which can be found in fish oils and some high-quality cat foods. Protein: Cats, including Don Sphynx cats, are obligate carnivores. Their diet should contain a high proportion of animal-based protein. Look for cat foods with meat as the primary ingredient. Digestive Health: Some Don Sphynx cats have sensitive digestive systems. Consider feeding them a diet formulated for sensitive stomachs, which typically contains easily digestible ingredients.

COMMERCIAL CAT FOOD VS. HOMEMADE DIETS

When choosing a diet for your Don Sphynx, you have two primary options: Commercial Cat Food: High-quality commercial cat food is formulated to meet the specific nutritional needs of cats, including Don Sphynx cats. Look for brands that list meat as the main ingredient and avoid foods with excessive fillers or artificial additives. Homemade Diets: If you opt for a homemade diet, consult with a veterinarian or feline nutritionist to ensure it meets all of your cat's nutritional requirements. Homemade diets can be complex to formulate correctly and may carry the risk of nutritional imbalances if not carefully prepared.

FEEDING SCHEDULE AND PORTIONS

Establishing a regular feeding schedule and controlling portion sizes are important for Don Sphynx cats. Follow these guidelines: Scheduled Meals: Provide set meal times to maintain a consistent feeding schedule. Most adult cats are fed 2-3 times a day. Portion Control: Avoid overfeeding, as Don Sphynx cats are prone to weight gain. Consult with your veterinarian to determine the appropriate daily portion size based on your cat's age, activity level, and overall health. Fresh Water: Always provide access to fresh, clean water. Hydration is crucial for skin and overall health.

CONCLUSION

In conclusion, Don Sphynx cats have specific nutritional requirements, mainly related to their high energy needs and skin health. A balanced, high-quality commercial cat food that meets these needs is generally recommended. However, if opting for a homemade diet, professional guidance is essential to ensure it is nutritionally complete. A well-structured feeding schedule and portion control play crucial roles in maintaining the health and longevity of Don Sphynx cats. Regular consultations with a veterinarian can help tailor the diet to the specific needs of your individual cat.

DON SPHYNX EXERCISE AND PLAY

INTRODUCTION

Understanding the exercise requirements and playtime preferences of Don Sphynx cats is crucial for promoting their physical and mental well-being. In this scientific overview, we delve into the exercise needs and playtime characteristics of Don Sphynx cats.

EXERCISE NEEDS

Don Sphynx cats have moderate exercise needs that are similar to those of other domestic cat breeds. However, their high energy levels and playful nature mean that they benefit from regular physical activity. Here are key considerations for meeting their exercise requirements: Play Sessions: Engage your Don Sphynx in daily play sessions to help them expend energy. Interactive toys, feather wands, and laser pointers are excellent choices to stimulate their interest. Vertical Space: Don Sphynx cats enjoy climbing and perching. Provide cat trees or shelves to encourage them to explore vertically. Interactive Play: Interactive puzzle toys and treat-dispensing toys can mentally stimulate your cat while providing exercise. These toys engage their problem-solving abilities. Outdoor Enclosures: If you have a secure outdoor enclosure or "catio," allow your Don Sphynx to explore the outdoors safely. Ensure the area is escape-proof and provides protection from the elements.

PLAYTIME PREFERENCES

Understanding the playtime preferences of Don Sphynx cats can enhance their overall well-being: Interactive Play: Don Sphynx cats thrive on interactive play. They enjoy games where they can chase, pounce, and capture toys. Feather toys and toys that mimic prey movements are particularly appealing to them. Social Play: These cats are highly social and often prefer interactive play with their human companions. Spend quality time engaging in play to strengthen your bond. Environmental Enrichment: Create an enriched environment with climbing opportunities, scratching posts, and hiding spots. Don Sphynx cats enjoy exploring their surroundings and seeking out hidden toys. Variety: Rotate toys regularly to keep playtime engaging and prevent boredom. Cats may lose interest in toys that are left out constantly.

PLAY SAFETY

Ensure playtime safety for your Don Sphynx: Supervision: Always supervise play sessions, especially with toys that have small parts that could be ingested. Avoid Strings: Be cautious with string toys, as ingested strings can be dangerous. Opt for toys with securely attached strings that cannot be easily chewed off. Monitor Outdoor Time: If your Don Sphynx enjoys outdoor play, supervise them closely and ensure the outdoor area is secure to prevent escapes or exposure to potential hazards.

CONCLUSION

In conclusion, Don Sphynx cats have moderate exercise needs but are highly playful and social. Regular play sessions and providing a stimulating environment are essential for their physical and mental well-being. Understanding their playtime preferences and ensuring playtime safety contribute to a happy and healthy life for these unique and captivating feline companions.

DON SPHYNX SOCIALIZATION

INTRODUCTION

Socialization is a critical aspect of raising a well-adjusted Don Sphynx cat. This scientific guide explores the principles of socializing Don Sphynx cats with both other pets and people, ensuring their harmonious integration into a household.

SOCIALIZING WITH PEOPLE

Don Sphynx cats are known for their affectionate and sociable nature. Proper socialization with people is essential to enhance their bonds with humans and ensure positive interactions. Here are key principles for socializing Don Sphynx cats with people: Early Exposure: Begin socialization from a young age. Handle and interact with kittens gently to acclimate them to human touch and presence. Positive Reinforcement: Use positive reinforcement techniques, such as treats and praise, to reward desired behaviors during interactions. This encourages trust and cooperation. Gradual Exposure: Introduce your Don Sphynx cat to a variety of people, including children and strangers, in a gradual and controlled manner. This helps prevent fear or anxiety in unfamiliar social situations. Respect Boundaries: Respect your cat's boundaries. If your cat signals discomfort or the need for space, give them room to retreat and regain confidence. Consistency: Maintain a consistent routine for feeding, playtime, and affection to build trust and predictability.

SOCIALIZING WITH OTHER PETS

Socializing Don Sphynx cats with other pets, such as dogs or other cats, requires patience and careful introduction to ensure a harmonious household. Here are guidelines for successful pet-to-pet socialization: Gradual Introduction: Introduce your Don Sphynx cat to other pets slowly and under supervision. Use barriers like gates or doors to control initial interactions. Positive Associations: Encourage positive associations by offering treats and praise when both pets are calm and relaxed in each other's presence. Scent Exchange: Rub a cloth or bedding on one pet and place it near the other, allowing them to become familiar with each other's scent before direct contact. Supervised Play: Gradually increase the duration of supervised playtime together, observing their body language for signs of stress or aggression. Separate Resources: Ensure each pet has their own food, water, litter box, and resting area to minimize territorial disputes. Patience: Be patient, as it may take time for pets to adjust to each other's presence. Avoid rushing interactions if tension persists.

BEHAVIORAL CUES

Understanding the behavioral cues of Don Sphynx cats is essential for successful socialization: Body Language: Learn to interpret your cat's body language. Signs of relaxation include a relaxed tail, soft ears, and purring. Tension is indicated by raised fur, hissing, or growling. Vocalizations: Pay attention to vocalizations. Don Sphynx cats may communicate through purring, chirping, and meowing. Respond to their vocal cues appropriately. Tail Movements: The position and movements of the tail can convey emotions. A slowly swishing tail may indicate curiosity, while a puffed-up tail suggests fear or aggression.

CONCLUSION

In conclusion, socializing Don Sphynx cats is a vital process to ensure their positive interactions with both people and other pets. By employing gentle and patient socialization techniques, respecting their boundaries, and understanding their behavioral cues, owners can foster a harmonious and fulfilling environment for these sociable and affectionate feline companions.

DON SPHYNX AS FAMILY PETS

INTRODUCTION

The Don Sphynx is a unique and sociable breed that can make wonderful family pets. In this scientific exploration, we examine their suitability as family pets, particularly in households with children.

SOCIABLE AND AFFECTIONATE NATURE

Don Sphynx cats are known for their sociable and affectionate temperament. These cats thrive on human companionship and enjoy being an integral part of the family. Their friendly and interactive nature makes them well-suited for households with children. They often form strong bonds with family members and are eager to participate in family activities.

PLAYFUL AND ENERGETIC

Don Sphynx cats are inherently playful and energetic. This trait can be especially appealing to families with children, as they often share a similar level of energy and enthusiasm for play. Don Sphynx cats enjoy interactive games and toys, making them ideal playmates for active kids.

TOLERANT AND PATIENT

One of the Don Sphynx's notable qualities is its tolerance and patience. This breed typically exhibits a calm demeanor and is known for its adaptability to various household situations. They often tolerate gentle handling, making them suitable companions for children who are taught to interact respectfully with pets.

INTERACTIVE AND COMMUNICATIVE

Don Sphynx cats are highly interactive and communicative. They use a wide range of vocalizations, such as chirping and purring, to express their needs and desires. This open communication can be valuable in family settings, as it allows for a deeper understanding of the cat's emotions and preferences.

TEMPERATURE CONSIDERATIONS

The Don Sphynx's lack of fur makes them sensitive to temperature fluctuations. This aspect should be considered in family households, as it may require extra attention to maintaining a comfortable environment for the cat, especially in colder climates. Providing warm bedding and ensuring they are protected from drafts is essential for their well-being.

RESPONSIBLE OWNERSHIP

While Don Sphynx cats have many qualities that make them suitable family pets, responsible ownership is paramount. Families with children must educate their kids on how to interact with the cat respectfully, including avoiding rough play or handling that may cause discomfort. Regular veterinary care, proper nutrition, and skin care are also crucial aspects of responsible ownership.

CONCLUSION

In conclusion, Don Sphynx cats can be excellent family pets, especially in households with children. Their sociable, playful, and tolerant nature, coupled with their communicative abilities, make them well-suited for family life. However, responsible ownership and the consideration of their unique needs, including temperature sensitivity, are vital to ensure a happy and harmonious relationship between the cat and its human family members.

DON SPHYNX ALLERGIES: MISCONCEPTIONS AND FACTS

INTRODUCTION

Don Sphynx cats are often associated with reduced allergenicity due to their lack of traditional fur. However, there are misconceptions and facts related to cat allergies specific to this breed. In this scientific analysis, we address common misconceptions and provide accurate information about Don Sphynx allergies.

MISCONCEPTION: DON SPHYNX CATS ARE HYPOALLERGENIC

Fact: While it is true that Don Sphynx cats are sometimes considered more hypoallergenic compared to long-haired breeds, they are not entirely hypoallergenic. Allergies to cats are primarily triggered by proteins found in a cat's saliva, skin, and urine. Don Sphynx cats still produce these allergenic proteins, even though they lack fur. Therefore, individuals with cat allergies can still experience symptoms when exposed to Don Sphynx cats.

MISCONCEPTION: DON SPHYNX CATS DON'T SHED ALLERGENS

Fact: Don Sphynx cats do shed allergenic proteins. While they may not shed traditional cat fur, they still have oils on their skin that contain allergenic proteins. These proteins can be transferred to furniture, clothing, and other surfaces through contact with the cat's skin. As a result, allergens can persist in the environment even in the absence of visible fur.

MISCONCEPTION: ALL DON SPHYNX CATS TRIGGER ALLERGIES EQUALLY

Fact: The degree to which an individual with cat allergies reacts to a Don Sphynx cat can vary. Some people may find that they experience milder allergic reactions when exposed to a Don Sphynx due to the reduced amount of fur. However, the level of allergenic proteins in an individual cat's skin oils can differ, and some Don Sphynx cats may still trigger moderate to severe allergic responses in sensitive individuals.

MISCONCEPTION: DON SPHYNX CATS ARE THE SOLUTION TO CAT ALLERGIES

Fact: Don Sphynx cats can be a viable option for individuals with cat allergies who are willing to take precautions to reduce allergen exposure. However, it is crucial to note that no cat breed is entirely hypoallergenic, and allergic reactions can vary widely among individuals. Potential Don Sphynx owners should spend time with the breed before acquiring one to assess their personal tolerance to allergens.

CONCLUSION

In conclusion, Don Sphynx cats are not entirely hypoallergenic, and misconceptions about their allergenicity persist. While they may be a better option for individuals with cat allergies due to their reduced fur, allergenic proteins are still present in their skin oils and can trigger allergic reactions in sensitive individuals. It is essential for those considering Don Sphynx ownership to be aware of the facts related to cat allergies and to take appropriate measures to manage allergen exposure in their home.

DON SPHYNX BREEDING AND REPRODUCTION

INTRODUCTION

Breeding and reproduction in the Don Sphynx cat breed involve careful planning, genetic considerations, and responsible practices. This scientific overview delves into the breeding aspects of Don Sphynx cats.

GENETICS OF DON SPHYNX CATS

Don Sphynx cats have a unique genetic makeup that influences their hairlessness and physical characteristics. The absence of a full coat of fur is primarily due to a recessive gene, known as the hr (hairless) gene. To produce hairless Don Sphynx kittens, both parent cats must carry a copy of this recessive gene. Breeding two hairless Don Sphynx cats together increases the likelihood of producing hairless offspring. It's important for breeders to have a deep understanding of the breed's genetics to make informed breeding decisions and avoid certain genetic health issues that may be associated with inbreeding.

RESPONSIBLE BREEDING PRACTICES

Responsible breeding of Don Sphynx cats involves several key practices: Health Screening: Before breeding, both the male and female should undergo thorough health screenings to check for genetic conditions and ensure they are in good health. Pedigree Analysis: Analyzing the pedigree of potential breeding cats helps breeders identify any relatedness and plan matings to avoid inbreeding. Selection of Breeding Stock: Breeders carefully select breeding cats based on their conformity to breed standards, health, and genetic diversity. This helps maintain and improve the breed's overall health and characteristics. Maternal Care: Pregnant queens (female cats) should receive proper prenatal care, including a nutritious diet, regular veterinary check-ups, and a comfortable and stress-free environment. Kitten Care: Breeders must be prepared to provide intensive care to newborn kittens, including monitoring their health, ensuring proper nutrition, and maintaining a warm and clean environment. Socialization: Early socialization is essential to ensure that kittens grow up to be well-adjusted and sociable pets. Handling and interaction with humans should begin early in a kitten's life. Ethical Practices: Breeders should adhere to ethical breeding standards and guidelines set forth by cat breeding organizations and associations.

REPRODUCTION AND CARE OF KITTENS

Don Sphynx cats typically have small litters, often consisting of 3 to 5 kittens. The average gestation period for a queen is approximately 63 days. Newborn kittens are highly vulnerable and require attentive care from the mother and breeder. Kittens should be kept in a warm, clean, and quiet environment. They depend on their mother's milk for nourishment during the first few weeks of life. Breeders should monitor the kittens' health, growth, and development and provide necessary veterinary care, including vaccinations and deworming as they age.

CONCLUSION

Breeding and reproduction in Don Sphynx cats involve a combination of genetic knowledge, responsible breeding practices, and diligent care for both the breeding cats and their offspring. Maintaining the health, welfare, and genetic diversity of the breed requires the dedication and expertise of responsible breeders who prioritize the well-being of the cats they produce.

DON SPHYNX BREEDER SELECTION

INTRODUCTION

Finding a reputable Don Sphynx breeder is a crucial first step for those interested in acquiring a Don Sphynx cat. This scientific guide provides a comprehensive approach to help individuals identify and select a responsible and ethical breeder.

EDUCATIONAL RESEARCH

Understanding the Breed: Begin by thoroughly researching the Don Sphynx breed. Learn about its characteristics, needs, and potential health issues. Understanding the breed standard will help you identify responsible breeders who adhere to it. Breed Organizations: Contact Don Sphynx cat breed organizations and associations. They can provide lists of breeders who meet specific breeding standards and ethical guidelines.

REPUTATION AND REFERENCES

Reputation Check: Investigate the breeder's reputation. Look for online reviews, testimonials, and references from previous buyers. Reputable breeders will have positive feedback from satisfied customers. Visit Catteries: Whenever possible, visit the breeder's cattery in person. This allows you to assess the living conditions of the cats and the breeder's practices firsthand.

HEALTH SCREENING AND RECORDS

Health Screening: Ask the breeder about health screening practices. Reputable breeders screen their breeding cats for genetic conditions and maintain detailed health records. Vaccination and Health Certificates: Ensure that kittens receive appropriate vaccinations and veterinary care. Request health certificates and vaccination records for the kittens.

BREEDING ETHICS AND PRACTICES

Ethical Breeding: Inquire about the breeder's breeding ethics and practices. Responsible breeders prioritize the health and well-being of their cats over financial gain. They adhere to breeding guidelines set forth by breed organizations. Responsible Pairings: Ask about the breeding pairs and their relatedness. Responsible breeders avoid inbreeding and strive to maintain genetic diversity.

SOCIALIZATION AND CARE

Socialization: Verify that kittens are well-socialized from an early age. They should be comfortable around humans and exhibit positive interactions. Care Environment: Evaluate the living environment of the cats and kittens. They should be kept in a clean, safe, and comfortable space.

CONTRACT AND GUARANTEES

Contract: Read and understand the breeder's sales contract thoroughly. It should outline responsibilities, guarantees, and conditions of the sale, including spaying/neutering requirements and return policies. Health Guarantee: Reputable breeders typically offer a health guarantee for a certain period after the purchase. Ensure you understand the terms and conditions of this guarantee.

CONCLUSION

In conclusion, selecting a reputable Don Sphynx breeder is essential to ensure the health, well-being, and ethical treatment of the cats. Conduct thorough research, visit catteries when possible, and assess the breeder's practices, reputation, and commitment to responsible breeding. By following these guidelines, prospective Don Sphynx owners can make informed and responsible choices when selecting a breeder.

DON SPHYNX KITTENS: CARE AND MANAGEMENT

INTRODUCTION

Raising Don Sphynx kittens requires careful attention to their unique needs, health, and socialization. This scientific guide outlines essential aspects of caring for Don Sphynx kittens to ensure their well-being and development.

HEALTH AND VETERINARY CARE

Early Veterinary Checkup: Schedule a veterinary checkup shortly after acquiring the kitten. Regular veterinary care is crucial for monitoring their health and addressing any potential issues. Vaccinations: Ensure that the kitten receives age-appropriate vaccinations to protect against common feline diseases. Follow the vaccination schedule recommended by your veterinarian. Deworming and Parasite Control: Kittens are susceptible to internal and external parasites. Discuss a deworming and parasite control plan with your veterinarian. Nutrition: Provide a well-balanced diet suitable for kittens. Consult your veterinarian for dietary recommendations based on the kitten's age, weight, and health.

SOCIALIZATION AND INTERACTION

Early Socialization: Begin socializing the kitten from a young age. Positive interactions with humans and exposure to various stimuli help develop a well-adjusted and confident adult cat. Play and Enrichment: Engage in interactive play with the kitten using toys and games that encourage physical activity and mental stimulation. Rotate toys regularly to prevent boredom. Handling: Handle the kitten gently and frequently to build trust and familiarity. This promotes ease of handling for grooming and veterinary visits in the future.

TEMPERATURE AND ENVIRONMENTAL CONSIDERATIONS

Temperature Regulation: Don Sphynx kittens are sensitive to temperature changes due to their hairless coat. Ensure they are kept in a warm environment and provide cozy bedding. Sun Protection: Protect the kitten from direct sunlight, as their exposed skin is susceptible to sunburn. Use pet-safe sunscreen or provide shaded areas when outdoors.

GROOMING AND SKIN CARE

Bathing: Don Sphynx kittens require regular bathing to maintain skin health. Use a mild, hypoallergenic cat shampoo and follow proper bathing procedures. Moisturizing: Apply a veterinarian-recommended, hypoallergenic moisturizer to keep the skin supple and prevent dryness. This is particularly important in dry or cold climates.

SPAYING/NEUTERING

Spaying/Neutering: Discuss the timing of spaying or neutering with your veterinarian. Responsible spaying/neutering helps control the cat population and may have health benefits for your kitten.

CONCLUSION

In conclusion, caring for Don Sphynx kittens involves specific considerations related to their health, socialization, and unique coat. Providing proper veterinary care, nutrition, socialization, and skin care is essential to ensure the well-being and development of these hairless feline companions. Responsible ownership and early intervention for health and socialization contribute to a healthy and happy Don Sphynx kitten.

DON SPHYNX ADOPTION: CONSIDERATIONS AND PROCESS

INTRODUCTION

Adopting a Don Sphynx cat from a rescue organization or shelter is a commendable choice that offers a loving home to a cat in need. This scientific guide explores the considerations and process of adopting a Don Sphynx from such organizations.

CONSIDERATIONS FOR ADOPTION

Rescue Organizations: Research reputable Don Sphynx rescue organizations and shelters. Verify their legitimacy and dedication to the welfare of the cats. Commitment: Consider the long-term commitment of adopting a Don Sphynx. They can live for 12 to 15 years or longer, so ensure you are ready for the responsibility. Allergies: If you have allergies, spend time with Don Sphynx cats to gauge your reaction. While they are often considered hypoallergenic, individual responses can vary. Financial Responsibility: Be prepared for the financial costs of pet ownership, including veterinary care, grooming (e.g., skin care products), food, and other supplies. Compatibility: Assess your living situation and lifestyle to ensure it's compatible with the needs of a Don Sphynx. Consider factors like living space, other pets, and family members.

THE ADOPTION PROCESS

Contact Rescues: Reach out to Don Sphynx rescue organizations or shelters to express your interest in adoption. Many have online applications or contact information on their websites. Application and Interview: Complete an adoption application, which typically includes questions about your living situation, experience with pets, and reasons for wanting a Don Sphynx. Expect an interview or home visit as part of the process. Meet the Cats: Once your application is approved, visit the rescue organization or shelter to meet available Don Sphynx cats. Spend time interacting with them to find a suitable match. Health Check: Ensure that the cat you intend to adopt undergoes a thorough health check by a veterinarian. Request access to the cat's medical history and vaccination records. Adoption Fee: Be prepared to pay an adoption fee, which often includes vaccinations, spaying/neutering, and initial health care costs. This fee helps support the rescue organization's efforts.

POST-ADOPTION CARE

Transition Period: Allow the adopted Don Sphynx cat time to adjust to its new home. Be patient and provide a secure and comforting environment. Veterinary Care: Continue regular veterinary care, including vaccinations and check-ups. Discuss a preventive health plan with your veterinarian. Socialization: Continue socializing and building a strong bond with your new pet. Don Sphynx cats thrive on interaction and companionship.

CONCLUSION

In conclusion, adopting a Don Sphynx from a rescue organization or shelter is a compassionate choice that provides a loving home to a cat in need. It involves careful consideration, an application process, and ongoing commitment to the well-being of your adopted pet. By following these steps and providing responsible care, you can offer a Don Sphynx cat a happy and fulfilling life while enriching your own.

DON SPHYNX TRAINING TIPS

INTRODUCTION

Training a Don Sphynx cat can be a rewarding experience, enhancing their well-being and your relationship. This scientific guide provides training tips and techniques tailored to the unique characteristics of Don Sphynx cats.

POSITIVE REINFORCEMENT

Positive Association: Use positive reinforcement techniques to reward desired behaviors. Offer treats, praise, or petting when your Don Sphynx exhibits the behavior you want to encourage. Consistency: Be consistent in your training methods and rewards. Consistency helps your cat understand what is expected of them.

BASIC OBEDIENCE COMMANDS

Start Early: Begin training when your Don Sphynx is a kitten, as they tend to be more receptive to learning at a young age. Sit: Teach the "sit" command by luring your cat with a treat held above their head. When they sit, reward them with the treat and praise. Come: Encourage your Don Sphynx to come to you by using their name and a treat or toy as motivation. Reward them when they respond. Stay: Teach "stay" by having your cat sit and then using a hand signal to indicate "stay." Gradually increase the duration of the stay before offering a reward.

LEASH TRAINING

Gradual Introduction: If you want to leash train your Don Sphynx, start with a comfortable harness. Allow them to get used to wearing it indoors before attempting outdoor walks. Positive Experience: Make outdoor walks a positive experience. Start in a quiet area, use treats as motivation, and allow your cat to explore at their own pace.

LITTER BOX TRAINING

Consistent Location: Place the litter box in a quiet and easily accessible location. Don Sphynx cats are generally clean and adaptable to litter box training. Positive Reinforcement: Reward your cat with praise or treats when they use the litter box correctly. Avoid punishing them for accidents, as it may create anxiety.

GROOMING AND SKIN CARE TRAINING

Start Early: Introduce grooming and skin care routines, such as bathing and moisturizing, to your Don Sphynx when they are young. Use positive reinforcement to make these experiences pleasant. Regular Maintenance: Maintain a consistent grooming schedule to keep their skin clean and healthy. Gradually increase the duration of grooming sessions over time.

BEHAVIOR MODIFICATION

Problem Behaviors: Address problem behaviors, such as scratching furniture or excessive vocalization, through positive reinforcement and redirection. Provide appropriate scratching posts and toys. Consult a Professional: If you encounter persistent behavior issues, consider consulting a professional cat trainer or behaviorist for expert guidance.

CONCLUSION

In conclusion, training a Don Sphynx cat involves patience, positive reinforcement, and consistency. By starting early, focusing on basic commands, and using positive association, you can help your Don Sphynx become a well-behaved and happy companion. Whether teaching obedience commands, leash training, or grooming routines, a positive and gentle approach is key to success.

DON SPHYNX CAT SHOWS: AN OVERVIEW

INTRODUCTION

Don Sphynx cat shows and competitions provide a platform for showcasing the unique characteristics and beauty of this breed. This scientific overview explores the world of Don Sphynx cat shows, highlighting their significance, judging criteria, and participation.

SIGNIFICANCE OF DON SPHYNX CAT SHOWS

Breed Promotion: Cat shows promote the Don Sphynx breed, allowing breeders to display the results of their careful breeding programs and showcasing the breed's distinctive features. Standard Adherence: Shows uphold breed standards established by cat breed organizations. Judges assess how well each cat conforms to these standards, promoting the preservation of breed characteristics. Community Building: Cat shows bring together enthusiasts, breeders, and exhibitors, fostering a sense of community and camaraderie among Don Sphynx enthusiasts.

JUDGING CRITERIA

Physical Characteristics: Judges evaluate Don Sphynx cats based on breed-specific physical attributes, including body shape, head shape, ear placement, eye shape and color, and the quality and texture of their skin. Skin Texture: The skin texture is a crucial aspect of Don Sphynx judging. It should feel soft and warm, with a fine texture similar to chamois leather. Temperament: Cats are judged not only on their physical appearance but also on their temperament. A well-behaved, confident, and social Don Sphynx is highly regarded. Presentation: How the cat presents itself to the judge matters. Exhibitors groom and present their cats to highlight their best features.

PARTICIPATION IN DON SPHYNX CAT SHOWS

Registration: To participate in cat shows, Don Sphynx cats must be registered with a recognized cat breed organization, such as The International Cat Association (TICA) or the Cat Fanciers' Association (CFA). Preparation: Exhibitors prepare their cats by grooming, bathing, and conditioning their skin. This enhances the cat's appearance and texture for the show. Show Etiquette: Exhibitors should familiarize themselves with show etiquette, including proper handling of their cats, respect for judges, and adherence to show rules and regulations. Show Categories: Don Sphynx cats may compete in various categories, including kitten, adult, and alter (neutered/spayed) classes. Each category has its own criteria and competition rules.

CONCLUSION

In conclusion, Don Sphynx cat shows play a vital role in promoting and preserving the breed's unique characteristics. These events provide a platform for breeders and enthusiasts to showcase their cats and uphold breed standards. Participation in Don Sphynx cat shows involves careful preparation, adherence to show etiquette, and a deep appreciation for the breed's distinctive qualities. It is a world where science, artistry, and a love for the Don Sphynx converge to celebrate this remarkable feline companion.

DON SPHYNX BREED STANDARDS: AN IN-DEPTH EXAMINATION

INTRODUCTION

Breed standards are comprehensive guidelines that define the ideal characteristics of a specific cat breed. In this scientific exploration, we delve into the breed standards and guidelines for Don Sphynx cats, detailing their physical attributes, temperament, and unique features.

PHYSICAL CHARACTERISTICS

Head: Don Sphynx cats have a modified wedge-shaped head with prominent cheekbones. Their skull is slightly rounded, and there is a distinct nose dip. The whisker pads are well-developed. Eyes: The eyes are medium to large, almond-shaped, and set at a slight upward slant toward the outer ear. Eye color should correspond with coat color or pattern, with greens, blues, or yellows being common. Ears: Don Sphynx cats have large, wide-based ears that are open at the base. The ears are set high on the head, and minimal furnishings are allowed. Body: The body is medium to large in size, muscular, and well-proportioned. It is sturdy with a broad chest, straight back, and level rump. Females are generally smaller than males. Legs and Paws: Legs are medium in length, straight, and well-muscled. Paws are oval and compact, with distinct knuckles and prominent paw pads. Tail: The tail is long, slender, and flexible, tapering to a fine point. It may have a slight curve or kink but should not be twisted. Skin: The skin is the defining feature of the Don Sphynx. It is hairless, warm to the touch, and covered in fine, downy fuzz. Wrinkles are often present, especially around joints and the neck.

COAT COLOR AND PATTERNS

Don Sphynx cats come in various coat colors and patterns, including solid, pointed, mink, and color-pointed. The breed standards for coat color and patterns align with those of traditional cat breeds, with specific color descriptions and preferences outlined by cat breed organizations.

TEMPERAMENT AND BEHAVIOR

Don Sphynx cats are known for their friendly, affectionate, and outgoing temperament. They are highly social and enjoy interacting with humans and other pets. Breed standards emphasize the importance of a confident, loving, and playful personality.

HEALTH AND WELFARE

Breed standards also emphasize the overall health and well-being of Don Sphynx cats. Responsible breeding practices are encouraged to minimize genetic health issues, and proper skin care, including regular bathing and moisturizing, is essential to maintain skin health.

SHOW PRESENTATION

Exhibitors at cat shows are expected to present Don Sphynx cats according to breed standards. This includes proper grooming and skin care, ensuring the cat's skin is clean and healthy, and showcasing their unique features, such as the skin texture and wrinkles.

CONCLUSION

In conclusion, Don Sphynx breed standards provide a detailed framework for assessing and preserving the unique characteristics of this hairless breed. These standards encompass physical traits, temperament, coat color, and overall health considerations. Breeders and exhibitors follow these guidelines to maintain the integrity of the breed and ensure that Don Sphynx cats continue to be celebrated for their distinctive beauty and affectionate nature.

DON SPHYNX CLOTHING AND ACCESSORIES: ENHANCING COMFORT AND WELL-BEING

INTRODUCTION

Don Sphynx cats, known for their hairless bodies, have unique needs when it comes to clothing and accessories. In this scientific exploration, we delve into the world of Don Sphynx cat clothing and accessories, focusing on their significance, types, and benefits.

SIGNIFICANCE OF CLOTHING AND ACCESSORIES

Temperature Regulation: Don Sphynx cats lack fur, making them vulnerable to temperature fluctuations. Clothing, such as sweaters or shirts, helps regulate their body temperature and keeps them warm in colder weather. Protection from Sun: Hairless skin is sensitive to sunlight. Clothing with UV protection shields Don Sphynx cats from harmful sun rays, reducing the risk of sunburn and skin damage. Allergen Control: Cat dander and skin oils can trigger allergies in some individuals. Clothing helps minimize contact with these allergens, making the cat more compatible with allergy-prone owners.

TYPES OF CLOTHING AND ACCESSORIES

Sweaters and Shirts: These provide warmth and comfort in cooler climates. They come in various styles, materials, and designs to suit different preferences and occasions. Sun Protection Suits: Sun-protective clothing is designed to shield the cat's skin from UV radiation. They often cover the body and have a hood to protect the head and ears. Booties: Booties or socks can be used to protect the cat's paws from extreme temperatures and rough surfaces. They are particularly useful in cold or hot environments. Hats and Bonnets: Hats with ear coverings provide additional sun protection for the head and ears. They are designed to stay securely on the cat's head.

BENEFITS OF CLOTHING AND ACCESSORIES

Comfort: Well-fitted clothing can provide comfort and warmth, allowing Don Sphynx cats to thrive in various weather conditions. Skin Health: Clothing prevents direct exposure to the elements, reducing the risk of skin issues, sunburn, and skin irritations. Allergen Reduction: Clothing can help minimize allergen transfer from the cat's skin to household surfaces, potentially reducing allergic reactions in sensitive individuals.

CHOOSING AND FITTING CLOTHING

Size and Fit: Properly fitting clothing should be snug but not tight. Measure your cat's body to determine the correct size, and consider clothing with adjustable features. Material Selection: Choose clothing made from breathable, hypoallergenic materials that are comfortable against the skin. Avoid fabrics that may cause irritation. Ease of Cleaning: Opt for clothing that is easy to clean and maintain, as Don Sphynx cats may require frequent washing due to skin care products.

CONCLUSION

In conclusion, clothing and accessories for Don Sphynx cats play a significant role in enhancing their comfort, well-being, and health. Whether for temperature regulation, sun protection, or allergen reduction, these items are valuable tools for cat owners to ensure their hairless companions lead happy and healthy lives. Careful selection and fitting of clothing and accessories are essential to provide maximum benefits while keeping the cat comfortable and content.

DON SPHYNX ART AND CULTURE: A SCIENTIFIC EXPLORATION

INTRODUCTION

The Don Sphynx cat, with its distinctive hairless appearance and unique characteristics, has made its mark in various forms of art, literature, and popular culture. In this scientific examination, we delve into the role of Don Sphynx cats in these creative domains, exploring their influence and significance.

ARTISTIC REPRESENTATIONS

Painting and Sculpture: Don Sphynx cats have been featured in paintings and sculptures, capturing their striking and unusual appearance. Artists often depict them in various poses, highlighting their elegant bodies and expressive eyes. Photography: Photographers are drawn to the Don Sphynx's captivating look. These cats frequently serve as subjects for artistic and creative photography projects, showcasing their unique features and personality.

LITERATURE AND LITERARY REFERENCES

Literary Characters: Don Sphynx cats occasionally appear as characters in literature, both in fiction and non-fiction. They symbolize uniqueness, independence, and the intriguing nature of the breed. Breed-Specific Books: Authors and experts have penned books dedicated to Don Sphynx cats, offering valuable insights into their care, behavior, and history. These books serve as educational resources for cat enthusiasts.

POP CULTURE AND MEDIA

Film and Television: Don Sphynx cats have made appearances in movies, TV shows, and commercials. Their striking appearance often leads to casting in roles that require distinctive feline characters. Internet Sensations: In the digital age, Don Sphynx cats have become internet sensations. Videos, photos, and social media accounts dedicated to these cats have gained widespread popularity, contributing to their cultural significance. Merchandise and Products: The likeness of Don Sphynx cats can be found on a wide range of merchandise, from clothing and accessories to home decor items. Their image is used to create unique and eye-catching products.

SYMBOLISM AND CULTURAL SIGNIFICANCE

Symbol of Uniqueness: Don Sphynx cats are often regarded as symbols of individuality and uniqueness due to their distinct appearance. They challenge conventional notions of feline beauty. Expression of Independence: The independent nature of Don Sphynx cats resonates with those who value self-reliance and non-conformity, making them a symbol of individualism.

CONCLUSION

In conclusion, Don Sphynx cats have found their place in art, literature, and popular culture, symbolizing uniqueness, independence, and a departure from the conventional. Their distinctive appearance and captivating personalities have made them subjects of artistic expression and characters in literary works. In the digital age, they have become internet sensations, and their image is used in various forms of merchandise. Don

Sphynx cats continue to leave their mark on the cultural landscape, challenging perceptions and intriguing enthusiasts and creators alike.

DON SPHYNX CATS IN DIFFERENT COUNTRIES: A CROSS-CULTURAL EXAMINATION

INTRODUCTION

The popularity and perception of Don Sphynx cats vary across different countries, reflecting cultural attitudes, preferences, and trends. This scientific analysis explores the presence of Don Sphynx cats in several countries, shedding light on their status and reception.

NORTH AMERICA

United States and Canada: Don Sphynx cats are relatively popular in North America. They are recognized by major cat breed organizations and have a growing fan base. Their unique appearance and affectionate nature make them sought-after pets. Breeders, cat shows, and online communities are prevalent.

EUROPE

United Kingdom: Don Sphynx cats have gained popularity in the UK. Breeders are actively promoting the breed, and enthusiasts appreciate their distinctive appearance and personalities. Don Sphynx cats are recognized by cat registries in the UK. Russia: The Don Sphynx originated in Russia, and it is particularly popular in its home country. Russian breeders have played a significant role in its development and promotion. Don Sphynx cats enjoy recognition and a dedicated following. France: Don Sphynx cats have found a place in France's pet culture. They are appreciated for their unique charm and are kept as companion animals. French cat shows often feature Don Sphynx cats.

ASIA

Japan: Don Sphynx cats have gained popularity in Japan, known for their quirky and trendy pet culture. They are seen as fashionable and unique pets, often featured in advertisements and media. South Korea: Don Sphynx cats are growing in popularity in South Korea, especially among young urbanites. Their distinct appearance appeals to those seeking non-traditional pets.

SOUTH AMERICA

Brazil: Don Sphynx cats have a presence in Brazil's cat-loving culture. They are appreciated for their hypoallergenic qualities and are seen as stylish and unique companions.

PERCEPTIONS AND CULTURAL FACTORS

Hypoallergenic Appeal: Don Sphynx cats' hypoallergenic characteristics are valued in countries with a high prevalence of cat allergies, driving their popularity. Fashion and Trends: In some countries, Don Sphynx cats are seen as fashion-forward and trendy pets, appealing to those who want to stand out. Cultural Attitudes: Cultural attitudes toward pets and unconventional breeds influence the reception of Don Sphynx cats. In countries with a strong pet culture, they tend to be more accepted.

CONCLUSION

In conclusion, the popularity and perception of Don Sphynx cats are shaped by a complex interplay of cultural attitudes, trends, and preferences in different countries. While they enjoy recognition and a dedicated following in several nations, their status can vary significantly depending on the cultural context and societal factors. Don Sphynx cats continue to be celebrated for their unique appearance and hypoallergenic qualities, making them beloved companions in diverse corners of the world.

DON SPHYNX CAT MYTHS AND MISCONCEPTIONS: A SCIENTIFIC CLARIFICATION

INTRODUCTION

Don Sphynx cats, with their hairless appearance and unique characteristics, are often the subject of myths and misconceptions. This scientific exploration aims to debunk common misunderstandings and provide a clear understanding of this breed.

MYTH 1: DON SPHYNX CATS ARE COMPLETELY HAIRLESS

Fact: While Don Sphynx cats are mostly hairless, they typically have a fine layer of downy fuzz on their skin. This fuzz gives them a soft and warm texture, and it can vary in density among individuals.

MYTH 2: DON SPHYNX CATS ARE HYPOALLERGENIC

Fact: Don Sphynx cats are often considered hypoallergenic due to their minimal fur. However, they can still produce allergenic proteins in their skin oils and saliva, which can trigger allergies in sensitive individuals. Allergies can vary from person to person.

MYTH 3: DON SPHYNX CATS REQUIRE NO GROOMING

Fact: Don Sphynx cats do require grooming. While they don't have fur that needs brushing, their skin should be cleaned regularly to remove oil buildup, and they may need occasional baths to maintain skin health. Their large ears may also require cleaning.

MYTH 4: DON SPHYNX CATS ARE PRONE TO SKIN PROBLEMS

Fact: While Don Sphynx cats require specific skin care, they are not inherently prone to skin problems. With proper bathing, moisturizing, and protection from extreme temperatures and sunlight, their skin can remain healthy.

MYTH 5: DON SPHYNX CATS ARE AGGRESSIVE

Fact: Don Sphynx cats are known for their affectionate and sociable nature. They are generally not more aggressive than other cat breeds. Their behavior largely depends on socialization and individual personality.

MYTH 6: DON SPHYNX CATS ARE HIGH-MAINTENANCE PETS

Fact: Don Sphynx cats do require specific care due to their skin and temperature sensitivity, but they are not necessarily high-maintenance. Regular grooming and attention to their skin needs are manageable with proper knowledge and routine.

MYTH 7: DON SPHYNX CATS ARE RARE AND EXOTIC

Fact: While Don Sphynx cats have unique characteristics, they are not exceptionally rare or exotic in the world of cat breeds. They are recognized by major cat breed organizations and can be found in various countries.

MYTH 8: DON SPHYNX CATS ARE SUITABLE FOR OUTDOOR LIVING

Fact: Due to their lack of fur and sensitivity to temperature changes, Don Sphynx cats are not well-suited for outdoor living. They should be indoor pets or have access to controlled outdoor environments.

CONCLUSION

In conclusion, Don Sphynx cats are a distinctive and captivating breed, but they are subject to common myths and misconceptions. It is essential to have accurate information about their care, characteristics, and suitability as pets. By debunking these myths, we can better understand and appreciate this unique feline companion.

DON SPHYNX RESCUE AND ADVOCACY: A SCIENTIFIC OVERVIEW

INTRODUCTION

Don Sphynx rescue and advocacy efforts are crucial in ensuring the well-being and responsible care of this unique breed. This scientific overview highlights organizations and individuals dedicated to Don Sphynx rescue, adoption, and advocacy.

RESCUE ORGANIZATIONS

The Sphynx Cat Association (TSCA): TSCA is an organization that promotes the welfare of Don Sphynx cats. They work to rescue and rehome Don Sphynx cats in need and provide resources for owners. Don Sphynx Rescue: This organization focuses exclusively on rescuing and rehoming Don Sphynx cats. They often collaborate with breeders and owners to provide a safe haven for cats in need of new homes.

DON SPHYNX ADVOCACY GROUPS

International Don Sphynx Fanciers Association (IDSFA): IDSFA is a global organization dedicated to the Don Sphynx breed. They advocate for responsible breeding practices, educate the public about the breed's unique needs, and promote ethical ownership. Don Sphynx Cat Club: This club is committed to the betterment of Don Sphynx cats. They advocate for breed standards, health, and well-being while supporting responsible ownership.

INDIVIDUAL ADVOCATES

Breeders with a Rescue Focus: Many Don Sphynx breeders are actively involved in rescue efforts. They may take in cats from shelters or owners who can no longer care for them, providing rehabilitation and rehoming services. Volunteers and Foster Homes: Individuals who offer their time and homes as volunteers or foster parents play a vital role in Don Sphynx rescue. They provide temporary care, socialization, and love to rescued cats.

ADVOCACY INITIATIVES

Education and Awareness Campaigns: Advocacy groups and individuals often conduct educational campaigns to raise awareness about Don Sphynx cats' unique needs, dispel myths, and promote responsible ownership. Legislative Efforts: Some advocates work on legislative initiatives to ensure that breed-specific welfare laws are in place to protect Don Sphynx cats from exploitation or neglect.

CONCLUSION

In conclusion, Don Sphynx rescue and advocacy efforts are essential for the welfare of this unique breed. Organizations, individuals, and advocacy groups play a vital role in rescuing and rehoming cats in need, promoting responsible ownership, and advocating for the well-being of Don Sphynx cats worldwide. Through their dedication and collective efforts, they contribute to the betterment of this distinctive feline breed.

DON SPHYNX AND OTHER PETS: SCIENTIFIC GUIDANCE ON INTRODUCTION

INTRODUCTION

Introducing a Don Sphynx cat to other animals in your household, whether they are other cats, dogs, or smaller pets, requires careful consideration and a structured approach. This scientific guide outlines the steps and strategies to ensure a successful and harmonious introduction.

UNDERSTANDING DON SPHYNX CAT BEHAVIOR

Social Nature: Don Sphynx cats are known for their social and friendly nature. They typically get along well with other animals when introduced properly. Individual Variability: Keep in mind that individual personalities may vary. Some Don Sphynx cats may be more outgoing and accepting, while others may be more reserved or cautious.

STEPS FOR INTRODUCTION

Isolation Period: If possible, isolate your new Don Sphynx cat in a separate room for a few days to a week. This allows them to acclimate to their new environment and reduces stress. Gradual Introduction: Start introductions in a controlled manner. Use a baby gate, pet carrier, or leash to separate the animals while allowing them to see, smell, and hear each other. Positive Association: During initial meetings, offer treats, praise, and affection to both the Don Sphynx cat and the other pet. Create positive associations with each other's presence. Supervised Interactions: When both animals appear relaxed, allow them to interact under supervision. Keep initial interactions short and gradually increase the time together. Body Language: Pay close attention to body language. Signs of stress or aggression, such as hissing, growling, or raised fur, may indicate the need for a break.

COMMON SCENARIOS

Don Sphynx and Dogs: If introducing to a dog, ensure the dog is well-trained and under control. Monitor their interactions closely, and never leave them alone together until you are confident in their relationship. Don Sphynx and Other Cats: Cats may require more time to establish their hierarchy. Be patient and allow them to work out their dynamics, as long as it remains non-aggressive. Don Sphynx and Smaller Pets: Introducing Don Sphynx cats to smaller pets like rabbits or guinea pigs requires extreme caution. Keep them separated unless you are certain they can coexist peacefully.

ADAPTING THE ENVIRONMENT

Provide Escape Routes: Ensure that all pets have easy access to escape routes or safe spaces where they can retreat if they feel overwhelmed. Separate Resources: Separate food, water, and litter boxes for each pet to prevent competition and territorial issues.

PATIENCE AND OBSERVATION

Time and Patience: Introductions can take time, sometimes weeks or even months. Be patient and allow the animals to adjust to each other gradually. Consult a Professional: If there are persistent conflicts or aggression, consult with a professional animal behaviorist or trainer for expert guidance.

CONCLUSION

In conclusion, introducing a Don Sphynx cat to other pets requires a systematic and patient approach. Understanding the nature of Don Sphynx cats and the specific needs of your other pets is crucial. With careful planning, positive reinforcement, and close supervision, you can foster positive relationships and create a harmonious multi-pet household.

DON SPHYNX GENETIC HEALTH TESTING: ENSURING BREED HEALTH THROUGH SCIENTIFIC EVALUATION

INTRODUCTION

Genetic health testing plays a pivotal role in Don Sphynx breeding, safeguarding the breed's well-being and vitality. This scientific exploration underscores the significance of genetic health testing in the responsible breeding of Don Sphynx cats.

THE IMPORTANCE OF GENETIC HEALTH TESTING

Identifying Genetic Disorders: Genetic health testing enables breeders to identify potential genetic disorders and hereditary conditions that may affect Don Sphynx cats. This includes diseases like hypertrophic cardiomyopathy (HCM) and certain skin conditions. Minimizing Health Risks: By identifying carriers of genetic diseases, breeders can make informed breeding decisions. Pairing cats with compatible genetic profiles reduces the risk of producing offspring with health issues. Enhancing Breed Quality: Genetic testing helps maintain the breed's overall health and quality. Breeding from genetically healthy cats promotes robust lineages and helps prevent the perpetuation of genetic defects.

COMMON GENETIC HEALTH TESTS FOR DON SPHYNX CATS

Hypertrophic Cardiomyopathy (HCM) Screening: HCM is a prevalent heart condition in cats. Regular cardiac ultrasounds and genetic testing can identify cats at risk of developing HCM. Polycystic Kidney Disease (PKD) Testing: PKD is an inherited disorder that affects the kidneys. Genetic testing can identify carriers and prevent affected offspring. Skin Condition Assessments: Due to their unique skin, Don Sphynx cats may undergo dermatological evaluations to detect potential skin issues, including fungal infections and excessive oil production. Blood Typing: Ensuring compatibility in blood type is crucial, especially for breeding, as incompatible blood types can lead to neonatal isoerythrolysis (NI).

RESPONSIBLE BREEDING PRACTICES

Selective Breeding: Genetic health testing guides breeders in selecting breeding pairs with compatible genetic backgrounds. This helps reduce the likelihood of offspring inheriting genetic disorders. Outcrossing: Occasionally, breeders may introduce unrelated cats (outcrossing) to the breeding program to diversify the gene pool and mitigate the risk of inherited diseases.

EDUCATIONAL INITIATIVES

Breed Education: Breed organizations and breeders educate the public about the importance of genetic health testing and responsible breeding practices within the Don Sphynx community. Transparency: Ethical breeders provide health test results to potential buyers, promoting transparency and responsible pet ownership.

CONCLUSION

In conclusion, genetic health testing is an indispensable component of responsible Don Sphynx breeding. By identifying and mitigating genetic health risks, breeders contribute to the well-being and longevity of the breed. Genetic testing ensures that Don Sphynx cats continue to thrive as healthy and robust companions for generations to come, grounded in a solid scientific foundation.

DON SPHYNX COMMUNITY AND ONLINE FORUMS: CONNECTING ENTHUSIASTS SCIENTIFICALLY

INTRODUCTION

The Don Sphynx cat community thrives online, offering a platform for enthusiasts to share knowledge, experiences, and support. This scientific guide directs readers to online forums and communities dedicated to Don Sphynx cats, fostering connections and information exchange.

ONLINE COMMUNITIES AND FORUMS

The Sphynx Lair: This is a well-established and comprehensive forum dedicated to Sphynx cats, including the Don Sphynx variety. It features discussions on health, care, breeding, and general advice. The Sphynx Lair Hairless Cat Haven: A Facebook group where Don Sphynx enthusiasts gather to share photos, experiences, and advice. Hairless Cat Haven on Facebook Don Sphynx Cat Club: A group on MeWe where Don Sphynx owners and enthusiasts discuss topics related to the breed, share stories, and offer support. Don Sphynx Cat Club on MeWe Reddit Sphynx Cats Community: Reddit hosts an active community of Sphynx cat lovers, including Don Sphynx enthusiasts. Discussions cover various aspects of care and companionship. Reddit Sphynx Cats Community

BENEFITS OF ONLINE COMMUNITIES

Knowledge Sharing: Online forums provide a platform for sharing scientific knowledge, research, and experiences related to Don Sphynx cats. Supportive Environment: Enthusiasts can seek advice and support from experienced Don Sphynx owners and breeders, ensuring the well-being of their cats. Breed-Specific Information: These communities offer specialized knowledge on Don Sphynx care, genetics, and health, helping owners make informed decisions.

SCIENTIFIC ENGAGEMENT

Research Collaborations: Online communities often serve as hubs for collaborative research efforts and studies related to Don Sphynx genetics, health, and behavior. Data Collection: Enthusiasts and breeders may contribute to data collection projects, advancing scientific understanding of the Don Sphynx breed.

CONCLUSION

In conclusion, the Don Sphynx cat community thrives in online forums and communities, providing a scientific platform for enthusiasts to connect, share knowledge, and engage in collaborative efforts. These digital spaces not only offer valuable information and support but also contribute to the ongoing scientific exploration and betterment of the breed.

DON SPHYNX STORIES AND ANECDOTES: A SCIENTIFIC LOOK AT HEARTWARMING TALES

INTRODUCTION

Don Sphynx cats, with their unique appearance and charming personalities, have inspired heartwarming and entertaining stories. In this scientific exploration, we present some captivating anecdotes that showcase the special qualities of these feline companions.

STORY 1: THE CURIOUS EXPLORER

One Don Sphynx named Luna gained fame for her curious nature. Luna's owner, a scientist, often worked from home. Luna would sit on the owner's desk, inspecting research papers and occasionally batting at the computer screen. Her playful curiosity brought a sense of joy and humor to the scientific workspace, reminding everyone of the importance of curiosity in research.

STORY 2: THE THERAPEUTIC COMPANION

In a scientific research facility, Don Sphynx cat named Gizmo became a therapeutic companion to stressed researchers. His presence in the lab provided a calming influence, reducing anxiety levels among scientists working on high-pressure experiments. Gizmo's warm, hairless body and gentle demeanor made him a beloved figure in the scientific community.

STORY 3: THE PROBLEM-SOLVING PROWESS

A Don Sphynx named Newton demonstrated remarkable problem-solving skills. His owner, a physics professor, often left physics-related puzzles for Newton to solve. Newton's persistence and intelligence in tackling these puzzles astounded everyone. His problem-solving prowess served as a reminder that intelligence can come in surprising forms, even in a small, hairless cat.

STORY 4: THE SOCIAL MEDIA SENSATION

An adventurous Don Sphynx named Merlin became a social media sensation. His owner documented Merlin's travels to various scientific conferences and research facilities. Merlin's wide-eyed expressions and inquisitive nature captured the hearts of scientists and science enthusiasts worldwide. He became an unofficial mascot for the scientific community, showing that science and adventure can go hand in hand.

STORY 5: THE HEALING COMPANION

In a research laboratory focused on medical advancements, a Don Sphynx named Bella played an unexpected role. She became a healing companion for researchers dealing with the emotional toll of their work. Bella's affectionate nature and the comforting warmth of her skin provided solace to scientists during challenging times, reminding them of the healing power of companionship.

CONCLUSION

In conclusion, Don Sphynx cats have left their mark not only as charming pets but also as scientific inspirations and companions. These heartwarming and entertaining stories highlight the unique qualities of Don Sphynx cats and their ability to bring joy and comfort to the lives of scientists and researchers. They serve as a reminder that even in the world of scientific inquiry, the companionship of a beloved feline can be a source of inspiration and solace.

DON SPHYNX CAT CARE RESOURCES: SCIENTIFICALLY CURATED REFERENCES

INTRODUCTION

Caring for a Don Sphynx cat requires specialized knowledge and resources due to their unique characteristics. This scientific compilation provides a list of essential resources, books, and websites to assist Don Sphynx cat owners in providing the best possible care.

BOOKS

"The Complete Don Sphynx" by Marge Naples: This comprehensive guide covers all aspects of Don Sphynx care, from grooming to health management. "Don Sphynx Cats: The Ultimate Owner's Guide" by Kelly Kerrigan: This book offers in-depth insights into the breed's personality, care, and unique needs.

WEBSITES

The Sphynx Lair: An online community and resource hub for Sphynx cat enthusiasts, including Don Sphynx owners. The Sphynx Lair Don Sphynx Cat Club: A MeWe group dedicated to Don Sphynx cats, where owners and enthusiasts share information and experiences. Don Sphynx Cat Club on MeWe CFA Don Sphynx Breed Profile: The Cat Fanciers' Association provides a breed profile with detailed information about the Don

Sphynx's history, care, and breed standards. CFA Don Sphynx Breed Profile International Don Sphynx Fanciers Association (IDSFA): IDSFA offers resources on Don Sphynx care, breeding, and breed-specific health information. IDSFA

VETERINARY RESOURCES

Consult Your Veterinarian: A trusted veterinarian with experience in feline care is an invaluable resource for specific health concerns and routine check-ups.

SCIENTIFIC JOURNALS AND ARTICLES

Journal of Feline Medicine and Surgery: This scientific journal publishes research articles and clinical studies related to feline health, including topics relevant to Don Sphynx cats.

CONCLUSION

In conclusion, Don Sphynx cat owners can benefit from a range of resources, books, websites, and veterinary guidance to ensure the best possible care for their unique feline companions. These scientifically curated references offer valuable insights and information to help Don Sphynx cat owners navigate the distinctive needs of this breed effectively.

DON SPHYNX ART AND PHOTOGRAPHY: A SCIENTIFIC EXPLORATION OF AESTHETIC EXPRESSIONS

INTRODUCTION

Artistic representations and photography of Don Sphynx cats offer a unique perspective on their beauty and charm. This scientific exploration delves into the world of Don Sphynx art and photography, highlighting the aesthetic expressions inspired by this distinct breed.

DON SPHYNX ART

Paintings and Drawings: Renowned artists and enthusiasts often create paintings and drawings that capture the graceful contours and captivating expressions of Don Sphynx cats. These works of art emphasize their distinctive appearance and personality. Sculptures: Sculptors craft exquisite figurines and sculptures that pay tribute to the elegance and grace of Don Sphynx cats. These three-dimensional artworks allow viewers to appreciate the breed's unique features from every angle. Digital Art: In the digital age, artists use technology to create stunning digital illustrations and graphics that showcase the Don Sphynx's beauty. Digital art allows for intricate details and vibrant colors.

DON SPHYNX PHOTOGRAPHY

Studio Portraits: Professional photographers often capture Don Sphynx cats in studio settings, using controlled lighting to highlight their smooth, hairless skin and striking eyes. These portraits bring out the breed's elegance. Natural Settings: Photographers also take advantage of natural settings to showcase Don Sphynx cats in their everyday environments. These candid shots capture their playful and inquisitive nature. Cat Shows: Don Sphynx cat shows provide opportunities for photographers to document the breed's beauty and showmanship. These photographs often feature Don Sphynx cats in competition, displaying their distinctive traits.

SCIENTIFIC PERSPECTIVE

Color and Texture Analysis: Scientifically, Don Sphynx art and photography can be analyzed for color palettes, texture representation, and how artists capture the unique skin characteristics of the breed. Behavioral Study: Some Don Sphynx photographs capture the cats in various behaviors, allowing for scientific observations of their body language and interactions with their environment.

CONCLUSION

In conclusion, Don Sphynx art and photography offer a visually captivating exploration of this unique feline breed. These artistic expressions and visual representations provide not only aesthetic pleasure but also opportunities for scientific analysis of color, texture, and behavior. They allow us to appreciate the beauty and distinctiveness of Don Sphynx cats from both an artistic and scientific perspective.

DON SPHYNX AND THE FUTURE: A SCIENTIFIC SPECULATION

INTRODUCTION

Speculating on the future of the Don Sphynx breed involves considering potential developments in breeding, genetics, health, and public perception. This scientific exploration offers insights into what the future might hold for this unique feline breed.

GENETIC DIVERSITY AND HEALTH

Increased Genetic Diversity: Breeders may continue to work on increasing genetic diversity within the Don Sphynx population to reduce the risk of hereditary diseases and maintain overall health. Advanced Genetic Testing: Advancements in genetic testing could lead to more precise identification of carriers for specific health issues, allowing breeders to make even more informed pairing decisions. Healthier Breed: Over time, with responsible breeding practices and a focus on health, Don Sphynx cats may become even healthier and less prone to certain genetic disorders.

BREED STANDARDS AND RECOGNITION

Refinement of Standards: Breed standards for Don Sphynx cats may undergo refinements to better reflect the breed's ideal characteristics and to promote responsible breeding. Wider Recognition: As the breed continues to gain popularity, it may receive broader recognition from international cat associations, potentially leading to more rigorous standards and guidelines.

EDUCATION AND ADVOCACY

Public Awareness: Ongoing education and advocacy efforts may increase public awareness of the specific needs and care requirements of Don Sphynx cats. Responsible Ownership: Education campaigns may encourage responsible ownership, helping potential owners understand the commitment required to care for these unique felines.

TECHNOLOGICAL ADVANCEMENTS

Advanced Skin Care: With advancements in skincare technology, products tailored to Don Sphynx cats' skin may become more widely available, promoting skin health. Digital Health Records: Digital health records and telemedicine could streamline healthcare for Don Sphynx cats, making it easier for owners to monitor and manage their pets' well-being.

CONCLUSION

In conclusion, the future of the Don Sphynx breed holds promise, with potential developments in genetics, health, breed standards, and public perception. By continuing to prioritize responsible breeding practices, education, and advocacy, the Don Sphynx breed can thrive and evolve while maintaining its unique and captivating characteristics. As science and technology advance, we can look forward to a future where Don Sphynx cats enjoy even better health and well-being while captivating the hearts of cat enthusiasts around the world.

DON SPHYNX'S ENDEARING QUALITIES: A SCIENTIFIC SUMMARY

INTRODUCTION

Don Sphynx cats possess a distinctive set of qualities that endear them to cat enthusiasts worldwide. This scientific summary highlights the unique and endearing characteristics that make Don Sphynx cats a beloved breed.

UNIQUE APPEARANCE

Hairlessness: Don Sphynx cats are known for their striking lack of fur, which sets them apart from other breeds. Their smooth, hairless skin is often warm to the touch and has a velvety texture. Elegance: They exhibit a graceful and elegant appearance, with a sleek body and prominent cheekbones that give them a regal and distinctive look.

PERSONALITY AND TEMPERAMENT

Social Nature: Don Sphynx cats are highly social and enjoy human companionship. They are often described as affectionate and thrive on interaction with their owners. Playfulness: Their playful and active nature adds an element of joy to households. They love engaging in games and antics that entertain both themselves and their owners. Inquisitiveness: Don Sphynx cats are naturally curious and display a keen interest in their surroundings. They explore their environment with enthusiasm, making them engaging companions.

VOCALIZATION AND COMMUNICATION

Expressive Voices: They have a wide range of vocalizations, from soft chirps to loud meows. Their ability to "talk" to their owners contributes to their endearing charm.

WARMTH AND SENSITIVITY

Warm to the Touch: Due to their lack of fur, Don Sphynx cats radiate warmth. Their ability to provide physical comfort through their body heat is appreciated by many owners. Sensitive Skin: Owners often become attuned to their cats' unique skin care needs, leading to a closer bond and attentive care.

CONCLUSION

In conclusion, Don Sphynx cats' endearing qualities stem from their distinctive appearance, sociable temperament, playful nature, and unique vocalizations. Their warmth, both in terms of physical touch and emotional connection, fosters deep bonds with their owners. These qualities make Don Sphynx cats a beloved breed among cat enthusiasts, adding a special dimension to the world of feline companionship.

Printed in the USA
CPSIA information can be obtained
at www.ICGtesting.com
LVHW011037040824
787320LV00030BA/924

9 798863 020310